ICS 11.020

SCM-C

世界中医药学会联合会康养产业分会

The Industrial Committee of Health Care of WFCMS

SCM-C 0053-2021

中医药健康养老服务规范

Specifications for Chinese Medicine Senior Care Service

分支机构标准

Committee Standard

2021-12-28发布实施

Issued & implemented on December 28, 2021

中医古籍出版社
Publishing House of Ancient Chinese Medical Books

图书在版编目（CIP）数据

中医药健康养老服务规范 / 世界中医药学会联合会康养产业分会编著 . -- 北京 : 中医古籍出版社 , 2025.2
ISBN 978-7-5152-2643-9

Ⅰ. ①中… Ⅱ. ①世… Ⅲ. ①中国医药学—应用—养老—社会服务—规范—中国 Ⅳ. ① D669.6

中国国家版本馆 CIP 数据核字 (2023) 第 068307 号

中医药健康养老服务规范
世界中医药学会联合会康养产业分会　编著

责任编辑　张　楚
封面设计　艺点锦秀
出版发行　中医古籍出版社
社　　址　北京市东城区东直门内南小街 16 号（100700）
电　　话　010-64089446（总编室） 010-64002949（发行部）
网　　址　www.zhongyiguji.com.cn
印　　刷　北京市泰锐印刷有限责任公司
开　　本　880mm×1230mm　1/16
印　　张　1.5
字　　数　40 千字
版　　次　2025 年 2 月第 1 版　2025 年 2 月第 1 次印刷
书　　号　ISBN 978-7-5152-2643-9
定　　价　38.00 元

目　　次

前　言

请注意本文件的某些内容可能涉及专利。本文件的发布机构不承担识别专利的责任。

本文件主要起草单位：北京市丰台区卫生健康委员会、世界中医药学会联合会国际标准部、世界中医药学会联合会康养产业分会、中卫中医药发展研究中心。

本文件参与起草单位：世界中医药学会联合会中医外治操作安全研究专业委员会、海南省中医院、河南中医药大学、中关村新智源健康管理研究院、乌鲁木齐市中医院、北京丰台右安门医院、北京市丰台区丰台社区卫生服务中心、北京市丰台区南苑社会福利中心、北京市丰台区西罗园社区卫生服务中心、北京市丰台区养合老年公寓、上海市针灸推拿综合研究会、中国农业科学院、中国人民解放军战略支援部队航天工程大学、中国航天基金会、云南省细胞生物技术研发中心、中佳银投资基金管理有限公司、蓝田城乡发展集团有限公司、上海浦东外商投资企业协会、鹰彤乾崧金融服务（深圳）有限公司、中国－菲律宾中医药中心、纳米比亚健康之路诊疗院、意大利中华医药学会、毛里求斯中国传统针推协会、迪拜草药治疗中心、德国曼海姆国立音乐与表演艺术大学、墨尔本艺术大学。

本文件主要起草人：杨丽雯、王丽丽、张涛、王晶、宾雪、李孟元、康锦伟、高明超、武留信、程亚伟、苏惠萍、周运峰、李昕雪、王婧雯、王萌萌。

本文件参与起草人：王令习、赵立强、王欣、姜长城、单玉伟、范亚泉、杨昶、李晓波、代宪明、王鸿翔、郑启明、贾福升、郭建安、赵颖慧、贺立新、郭俣浩、王道龙、王旭、李军、李明、钟煜朝、靖猛。

引　言

发展中医药健康养老服务，是应对人口老龄化、加快推进健康产业发展、全方位全周期保障人民健康的重要举措，对满足老年人养生保健和看病就医等健康需求，提高生命生活质量，释放养老消费潜力，以及稳增长、促改革、调结构、惠民生和全面建成小康社会，具有重要意义。

中医药健康养老服务规范

1 范围

本文件规定了针对老年人使用的中医药健康养老服务的术语与定义、基本要求、服务内容、服务流程和服务评价与持续改进的要求。

本文件适用于提供中医药健康养老服务的医疗机构和非医疗机构。

2 规范性引用文件

下列文件中的内容通过文中的规范性引用而构成本文件必不可少的条款。其中，注日期的引用文件，仅该日期对应的版本适用于本文件；不注日期的引用文件，其最新版本（包括所有的修改单）适用于本文件。

GB/T 21709.1 针灸技术操作规范 第 1 部分：艾灸

GB/T 21709.5 针灸技术操作规范 第 5 部分：拔罐

GB/T 21709.9 针灸技术操作规范 第 9 部分：穴位贴敷

GB/T 21709.20 针灸技术操作规范 第 20 部分：毫针基本刺法

GB/T 21709.21 针灸技术操作规范 第 21 部分：毫针基本手法

GB/T 21709.22 针灸技术操作规范 第 22 部分：刮痧

GB/T 29353 养老机构基本规范

GB 50763 无障碍设计规范

MZ/T 032 养老机构安全管理

JGJ 450 老年人照料设施建筑设计标准

3 术语和定义

下列术语和定义适用于本文件。

中医药健康养老服务

运用中医药理念、方法和技术，为老年人提供连续的保养身心、预防疾病、改善体质、诊疗疾病、增进健康的中医药健康管理服务和医疗服务。

4 基本要求

4.1 一般要求

4.1.1 各项服务应符合老年人生理、病理特点和身心需求。
4.1.2 应尊重老年人的生活习惯、宗教信仰和民族习俗，保护老年人的隐私。
4.1.3 为老年人提供服务过程中应保证老年人的身心健康、饮食卫生和财产安全。

4.2 服务机构

4.2.1 各机构应合法、合规，具备相应的资质证书。
4.2.2 各机构应设置老年人中医药健康服务的场所，配备相关设施设备，并能提供老年人所需的基本服务。
4.2.3 老年人居室配置的设施设备、用具安全及无障碍设施应符合GB/T 29353、GB 50763、JGJ 450、MZ/T 032相关规定。
4.2.4 各机构应定期维护开展中医药健康养老服务相关的设施设备，确保其能正常使用。
4.2.5 各机构应在服务过程中符合院感防控和疫情防控的相关要求，避免交叉感染。
4.2.6 各机构应建立中医药健康养老服务的相关管理制度，包括但不限于：人员管理、服务规范、评价与持续改进制度等。
4.2.7 各机构应制定老年人中医药健康养老服务计划，并有相应的实施方案。
4.2.8 各机构开展中医药健康养老服务应配备相适应的管理人员、专业技术人员和服务人员，人员数量配比应满足服务需求。
4.2.9 各机构可根据老年人需求及实际情况，开展上门中医药健康养老服务。有条件的机构可开展远程医疗服务，以辅助诊断与治疗。

5 服务内容

提供中医药健康养老服务的机构应当提供的服务项目包括但不限于：
——中医体质辨识与评估；
——中成药 / 中药饮片 / 中药配方颗粒剂；
——针刺；
——按摩；
——刮痧；
——拔罐；
——艾灸；
——耳穴压豆；
——放血疗法；
——穴位贴敷；
——穴位保健；
——中药熏洗；
——个性化起居养生；

——膳食调养；
——情志调养；
——传统体育运动；
——中医健康教育与咨询等。

6 服务要求

6.1 各机构应根据老年人的实际需求，为其提供医疗、预防、康复、安宁疗护和健康管理等中医药特色全方位健康服务。

6.2 中医药健康养老服务应根据服务项目选择具备相应资质的医护人员和相关服务人员开展，或者在相应资质的医护人员的监督、指导下开展。饮食制作人员应持有健康证，并经过专业培训且合格。

6.3 各机构应根据老年人实际需要，对于行动不便的老年人，应有家人知情同意或专人配合完成。在老年人及其家属共同参与下，制定个性化服务计划，并由本人或家属签署知情同意书及风险告知书。定期检查老年人的体质和心理变化，定期评估，及时调整服务项目及实施方案。

6.4 各机构可根据实际情况使用网络服务平台，以便及时了解中医药健康养老服务的开展情况，加强远程便捷程度和干预效果。

6.5 中医药健康养老服务操作人员为老年人提供相应医疗服务项目时：
——针灸技术操作应符合 GB/T 21709.20 及 GB/T 21709.21 的规定；
——刮痧技术操作应符合 GB/T 21709.22 的规定；
——拔罐技术操作应符合 GB/T 21709.5 的规定；
——艾灸技术操作应符合 GB/T 21709.1 的规定；
——穴位敷贴技术操作应符合 GB/T 21709.9 的规定等。

6.6 服务人员所使用的器具用具应符合相关的规定和要求。

6.7 各机构对各项中医健康养老服务措施实施过程中出现的不良事件应制定预案。

7 服务流程

7.1 中医药健康养老服务具体服务流程应包括服务接待、老年需求及能力评估、制定服务计划、签订服务协议、建立服务档案、提供中医药健康养老服务、服务反馈等。

7.2 接待服务应包括了解并记录服务对象老年人的基本情况、健康状况、疾病史等内容，介绍机构能够提供的服务内容，为服务对象匹配合适的服务人员并对老年人服务需求信息及时给予反馈。

7.3 各机构应定期为有需求的老年人开展中医健康状态辨识评估，根据评估结果给予相应的中医药健康指导，制定相应的中医药健康养老服务计划。

7.4 根据服务计划与老年人（或其代理人）签订服务协议。主要条款包括但不限于：
——机构名称、住所、法定代表人或主要负责人、联系方式；
——老年人（或其代理人）、经常联系人的姓名、住址、身份证明、联系方式；
——当事人的权利和义务；
——服务内容和服务方式；
——服务期限和地点；

——协议变更、解除与终止的条件；
——违约责任；
——意外伤害责任认定和争议解决方式；
——当事人协商一致的其他内容。

7.5 将服务过程中形成的文件、记录、协议等及时汇总、分类和归档，为老年人建立服务档案。档案资料包括但不限于：

——老年人健康档案相关资料；
——老年人护理需求评估报告；
——具备中医服务资质的机构出具的中医评估报告；
——服务计划表；
——各项医疗卫生和养老服务记录；
——服务协议。

8 服务评价与持续改进

8.1 评价内容与方式

8.1.1 中医药健康养老服务评价宜采取日常检查、定期检查、不定期抽查、专项检查等方式，进行服务质量检查，包括但不限于下列内容：

——服务质量；
——服务项目；
——服务人员；
——服务满意度（线上、线下填写）；
——工作记录与归档情况。

8.1.2 中医药健康养老服务评价宜由第三方专业机构或专家进行。

8.2 持续改进

8.2.1 机构服务人员在中医药健康养老服务中发现的问题，应及时报告相关管理部门。

8.2.2 机构应对收集的中医药健康养老相关意见和建议、自查报告和第三方评价情况进行分析，查找问题原因，采取有效可行措施，以实现持续改进。

8.2.3 机构应从服务的适应性、可及性和服务方法、技术手段和质量、水平、能力等方面进行自查，并持续改进。

参考文献

［1］王国强，杨文明．中医药健康养老服务战略研究报告［M］．北京：中国中医药出版社．2019.
［2］上海市“治未病”发展研究中心．养老机构中医适宜技术手册［M］．上海：上海交通大学出版社．2017.

Foreword

Attention is drawn to the possibility that some of the elements of this standard may be the subject of patent rights. World Federation of Chinese Medicine Societies (WFCMS) shall not be held responsible for identifying any or all such patent rights.

Main Drafting Units: Health Commission of Fengtai District of Beijing, Department of International Standardization of WFCMS, Industrial Committee of Health Care of WFCMS, China Health Development and Research Institute of Chinese Medicine.

Drafting Units Participated: Specialty Committee of Safety Research on TCM External Treatment Procedures of WFCMS, Hainan Provincial Hospital of TCM, Henan University of Chinese Medicine, Zhongguancun Xinzhiyuan Health Management Institute, Urumqi Hospital of Traditional Chinese Medicine, Beijing Fengtai Youanmen Hospital, Fengtai Community Health Service Center of Fengtai District of Beijing, Nanyuan Social Welfare Center of Fengtai District of Beijing, Xiluoyuan Community Healthcare Center of Fengtai District of Beijing, Yanghe Apartment for the Elderly of Fengtai District of Beijing, Shanghai Comprehensive Research Association of Acupuncture and Massage, Chinese Academy of Agricultural Sciences, Space Engineering University of Strategic Support Force of PLA, China Space Foundation, Yunnan Cell Biotechnology Research and Development Center, Zhongjiayin Investment Fund Management (Shenzhen) Co.,LTD, Lantian Urban and Rural Development Group Co.,LTD , Shanghai Pudong Association of Enterprises with Foreign Investment, Yintone Financial Services (Shenzhen) Co.,LTD, China-Philippines TCM Center, Namibia Healthy Way Traditional Chinese Medicine Clinic, Italian Institute of Traditional Chinese Medicine, Mauritius-China Traditional Acupuncture Association, Dubai Herbal and Treatment Center, Staatliche Hochschule für Musik und Darstellende Kunst Mannheim, Melboure Art College.

Main drafters: Yang Liwen, Wang Lili, Zhang Tao, Wang Jing, Bin Xue, Li Mengyuan, Kang Jinwei, Gao Mingchao, Wu Liuxin, Cheng Yawei, Su Huiping, Zhou Yunfeng, Li Xinxue, Wang Jingwen, Wang Mengmeng.

Participating Drafters: Wang Lingxi, Zhao Liqiang, Wang Xin, Jiang Changcheng, Shan Yuwei, Fan Yaquan, Yang Chang, Li Xiaobo, Dai Xianming, Wang Hongxiang, Zheng Qiming, Jia Fusheng, Guo Jian'an, Zhao Yinghui, He Lixin, Guo Minhao, Wang Daolong, Wang Xu, Li Jun, Li Ming, Zhong Yuchao, Jing Meng.

Introduction

The development of Chinese medicine health care service is an important initiative in response to population aging, and for speeding up the construction of health industry to safeguard the health of people in full-life cycles targeting all health influencing factors. It is of great significance to meet healthy needs of the elderly such as preserving health and seeking for medical advice, to improve life quality and to unleash the consumption potential of senior care. It also contributes to maintaining stable growth, advancing reform, making structural adjustments, improving living standards and building a moderately prosperous society in all respects.

Specifications for Chinese Medicine Senior Care Service

1 Scope

This document specifies terms and definitions, basic requirements, and service contents, process and evaluation and the requirements on consistant improvement of Chinese Medicine Senior Care Service.

This document applies to medical and non-medical organizations providing Chinese medicine health care services.

2 Normative references

The following referenced documents are indispensable for the application of this document. For dated references, only the edition cited applies. For undated references, the latest edition of the referenced document (including any amendments) applies.

GB/T 21709.1 Standardized Manipulations of Acupuncture and Moxibustion–Part 1: Moxibustion

GB/T 21709.5 Standardized Manipulations of Acupuncture and Moxibustion–Part 5: Cupping Therapy

GB/T 21709.9 Standardized Manipulations of Acupuncture and Moxibustion–Part 9: Acupoint Paste

GB/T 21709.20 Standardized Manipulations of Acupuncture and Moxibustion–Part 20: Basic Techniques of Filiform Needle

GB/T 21709.21 Standardized Manipulations of Acupuncture and Moxibustion–Part 21: Filiform Needle Manipulation by Basic Applying Technique

GB/T 21709.22 Standardized Manipulations of Acupuncture and Moxibustion–Part 22: Scraping Therapy

GB/T 29353 Basic Standard for Senior Care Organization

GB 50763 Codes for Accessibility Design

MZ/T 032 Safety Management for Senior Care Organization

JGJ 450 Standard for Design of Care Facilities for the Aged

3 Terms and definitions

For the purpose of this document, the following terms and definitions apply.

Chinese medicine senior care service

By applying Chinese medicine thoughts, methods and techniques, it continuously provides Chinese medicine health management and medical services for the elderly in order to maintain health of both body and mind by preventing diseases and improving body constitution, and to diagnose and treat diseases.

4 Basic requirements

4.1 General requirements

4.1.1 All services shall cater to the physiological and pathological characteristics as well as the physical and mental needs for the elderly.

4.1.2 It shall respect living habits, religious faith and ethnic custom of the elderly and protect their privacy.

4.1.3 During the service delivery for the elderly, it shall ensure the physical and psychological health, and food and property safety of the elderly.

4.2 Organizations

4.2.1 Institutions shall obey the law and regulations, and obtain corresponding certificates.

4.2.2 Institutions shall provide places for delivery Chinese medicine health care services for the elderly equipped with related facilities, and provide basic services that the elderly needs.

4.2.3 The facilities, utensil safety and barrier-free facilities in the room of the elderly shall conform to the relevant provisions of GB/T 29353, GB 50763, JGJ 450, and MZ/T 032.

4.2.4 Institutions shall regularly maintain the facilities applied for delivering Chinese medicine health care services to ensure their normal use.

4.2.5 Institutions shall obey the relevant requirements of hospital infection prevention and epidemic control and prevention during service delivery in order to avoid cross-infection.

4.2.6 Institutions shall establish relevant management systems for Chinese medicine health care service, including but not limited to: personnel management, service specification, evaluation and continuous improvement system, etc.

4.2.7 Institutions shall make Chinese medicine health care service plans for the elderly with corresponding implementation programs.

4.2.8 Institutions that provide services of Chinese medicine health care for the elderly shall be equipped with appropriate management, professional and service personnel, and the number and proportion of each kind of personnel shall meet the needs of the service.

4.2.9 Institutions can provide door-to-door Chinese medicine health care services according to the needs and actual situation of the elderly. They can provide telemedicine services to assist in disease diagnosis and treatment if possible.

5 Service contents

The services that organizations shall provide include but not limited to:

——recognition and evaluation of body constitution in Chinese medicine;

——Chinese patent drugs/Chinese medicine decoction pieces/Chinese medicine formula granules;

—— acupuncture;

——tuina;

——scraping therapy;

——cupping therapy;

—— moxibustion;

—— auricular point pressing therapy;

—— blood-letting therapy;

—— acupoint paste;

—— health care with acupoint;

—— Chinese medicine fumigation and washing therapy;

—— individualized health preservation in daily life;

—— dietary regulation;

—— emotional regulation;

—— traditional physical exercises;

—— Chinese medicine health education and consultation, etc.

6 Service requirements

6.1 Based on the actual needs of the elderly, institutions shall provide comprehensive health services with Chinese medicine characteristics, covering medical treatment, prevention, rehabilitation, hospice care and health management.

6.2 Qualified medical personnel with corresponding and relevant certifications shall be selected, or personnel carry out service under the supervision and guidance of the corresponding qualified medical personnel, according to the service items in Chinese medicine senior care services. Each catering personnel shall have a health certificate and be professionally trained and qualified.

6.3 Institutions shall take the actual needs of the elderly into consideration. For the elderly with disabilities or inconvenient in movement, institutions shall have family informed consent or specific personnel to assist. With the participation of the elderly and their families, a personalized service plan shall be formulated, with a sign on the informed consent and risk notice. The service plan shall be regularly evaluated and adjusted based on their physical and psychological changes.

6.4 Institutions shall make full use of the network service platform according to the actual situation, so as to timely master the implementation of Chinese medicine senior care services, and shall improve remote convenience and intervention effect of network service.

6.5 Medical personnel carrying out items in Chinese medicine senior care services shall:

——the practice of acupuncture shall be in accordance with GB/T 21709.20 and GB/T 21709.21;
——the practice of guasha shall accord with GB/T 21709.22;
——the practice of cupping shall comply with GB/T 21709.5;
——the practice of moxibustion shall be in accordance with GB/T 21709.1;
——the practice of acupoint plaster shall comply with GB/T 21709.9.

6.6 The appliances and apparatus used by the service personnel shall comply with relevant regulations and requirements.

6.7 Institutions shall formulate contingent plans in case of the occurrence of adverse events during the implementation process and measures of various Chinese medicine health senior care service.

7 Service process

7.1 The specific process for Chinese medical health senior care services shall include reception service, evaluation of needs and ability of the elderly, formulation of service plan, signing of the service agreement, setting-up of service files, implementation of Chinese medicine health care service, service feedback, etc.

7.2 The reception service shall include obtaining and recording the basic situation, health status and disease history of the elderly, introducing the service content that the organization can provide to the elderly, matching suitable service personnel for the elderly, and timely updating the service needs information of the elderly.

7.3 Institutions shall regularly carry out the identification and assessment of the Chinese medicine health status for the elderly with corresponding needs, give the Chinese medical health guidance according to the evaluation results, and formulate the Chinese medicine senior care service plans.

7.4 Sign a service agreement with the elderly (or their families) according to the service plan. The main terms include, but are not limited to, the following:

——institution name, address, legal representative or principal person in charge, contact information;
——name, address, personal identity certification, contact information of the elderly (or their families) and regular contacts;
——rights and obligations of the parties;
——service content and service mode;
——service duration and location;
——conditions for change, dissolution and termination of agreement;
——the responsibility for breach of agreement;
——identification of accidental injury liability and dispute settlement methods;
——other contents agreed by the two parties concerned.

7.5 The documents, records and agreements formed in the service process will be summarized, classified and filed in time to establish service files for the elderly. Archive materials include but are not limited to:

——health records related to the elderly;

——assessment report of senior care requirements;
——Chinese medicine evaluation report issued by institutions with the qualification certification;
——service schedule;
——records of medical items, health care and senior care services;
——service agreement.

8 Service assessment and consistent improvements

8.1 Assessment content and methods

8.1.1 The assessment to the Chinese medicine health senior care service shall be carried out by routine inspection, regular inspection, spot inspection, special inspection to supervise service quality. The contents include but not limited to the followings:

——service quality;
——service items;
——service personnel;
——service satisfaction (online and offline);
——work records and archives.

8.1.2 The assessment to the Chinese medicine health senior care service shall be carried out by third-party professional institutions or experts.

8.2 Consistent improvements

8.2.1 Service personnel shall report problems found in Chinese medicine health senior care service to the relevant management departments in time.

8.2.2 Institutions shall analyze opinions and suggestions on Chinese medicine health senior care service, self-examination reports and third-party assessment report, find out the causes of the problems, and take effective and feasible measures to achieve consistent improvements.

8.2.3 The institution shall conduct self-inspection on the adaptability, accessibility and methods, technical means, quality, level and ability of the service, and continuous improvement.

Bibliography

[1]Wang GQ, Yang WM. Strategic research report on Chinese medicine health senior care services [M] . Beijing: China Press of Chinese Medicine, 2019.

[2] Shanghai "Preventive Treatment of Disease" Development and Research Center. Manual for Chinese medicine techniques in senior care institutions [M] . Shanghai: Shanghai Jiao Tong University Press, 2017.